Frightfully Fun
HALLOWEEN
ACTIVITY BOOK

Tony J. Tallarico

Dover Publications, Inc.
Mineola, New York

Bibliographical Note

Frightfully Fun Halloween Activity Book is a new work, first published by
Dover Publications, Inc. in 2009.

International Standard Book Number

ISBN-13: 978-0-486-47131-0
ISBN-10: 0-486-47131-4

Manufactured in the United States by Courier Corporation
47131403
www.doverpublications.com

NOTE

Just about everyone has a favorite holiday. Maybe *your* favorite is the subject of this frightfully fun-filled book: Halloween! Whether it's dressing up in a costume, trick-or-treating, or decorating a pumpkin, Halloween has something for everyone.

Look inside and you'll find lots of challenging puzzles and activities. Follow a set of footprints through a maze, circle a mummy that's different from the rest, use codes to answer ghostly riddles, draw your own mystery pictures, and unscramble Halloween words using clever clues—these are just a few of the challenges that await you.

You don't have to wait until October 31 to celebrate Halloween. Be prepared for tons of fun, and make sure that you have your colored pencils, markers, or crayons handy, because when you've finished the puzzle pages, you can have even more fun coloring them in. There's a Solutions section, beginning on page 36, but don't peek at the answers until you've tried your hardest. Have fun!

A BATTY RIDDLE-MAZE

Travel through this bat maze to answer the following riddle.

"WHICH IS MY FAVORITE HOLIDAY?"

START

THANKSGIVING

HALLOWEEN

APRIL FOOL'S

A COUPLE OF SCARECROWS

Only 2 of these Halloween scarecrows have identical twins on this page.
Find the 2 matching pairs and draw lines between them.

A.

B.

C.

D.

E.

F.

G.

THESE SCARECROWS ALL LOOK THE SAME TO ME!

A GHOSTLY MAZE

Which ghost will you visit? Choose the correct path and find out.

A PUMPKIN FACT

Use this special chart to decode the fact below.

A TO Z DOT-TO-DOT

Complete this alphabet dot-to-dot picture.

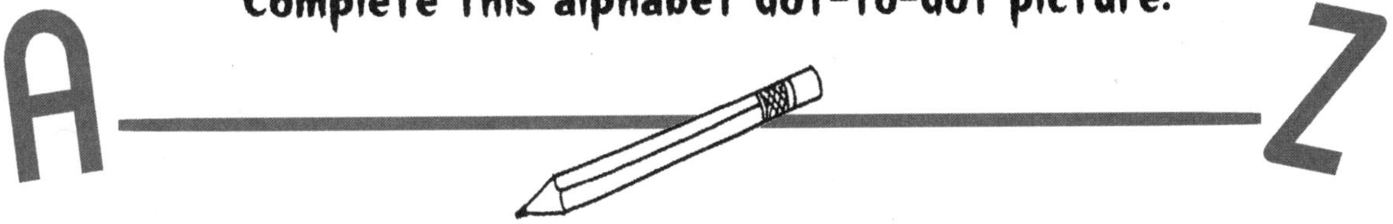

A ————————— Z

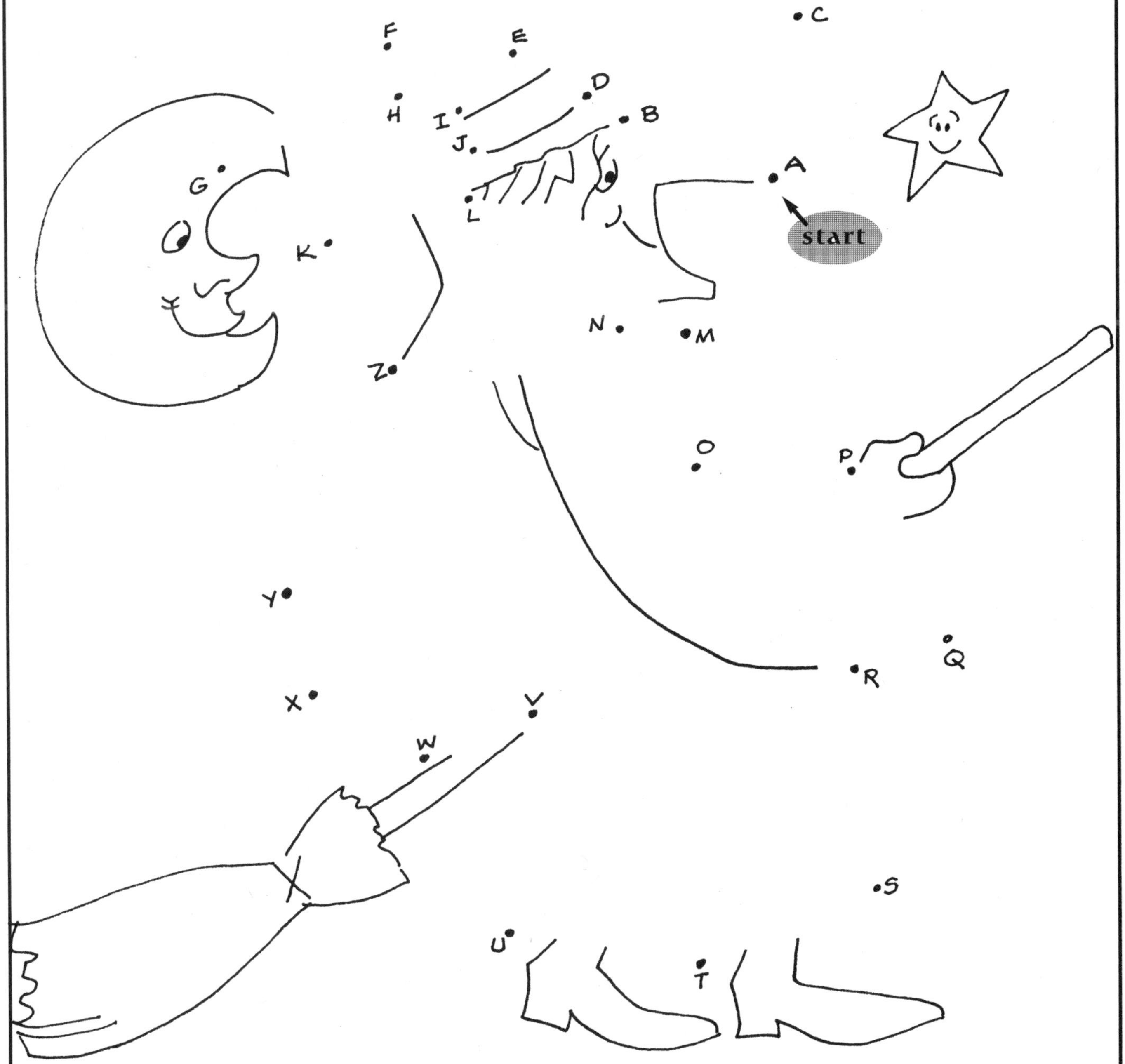

F
E
C

H
I
D
B
J
A
start

G
L
K

N
M
Z

O
P

Y
R
Q

X
V
W

S

U
T

ALL WRAPPED UP IN HIMSELF

One of these mummies is different from the rest.
Find and circle him!

#1

#2

#3

#4

#5

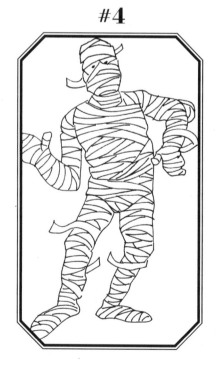

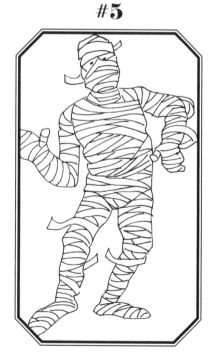

CIRCLE-A-WORD

Find and circle the following hidden Halloween words in this puzzle.

COSTUME
EERIE
FUNNY
GHOSTLY
GHOUL
GOBLIN
HAUNT
LAUGH
MASQUERADE
OCTOBER
SKELETON
SPOOKY
WITCH

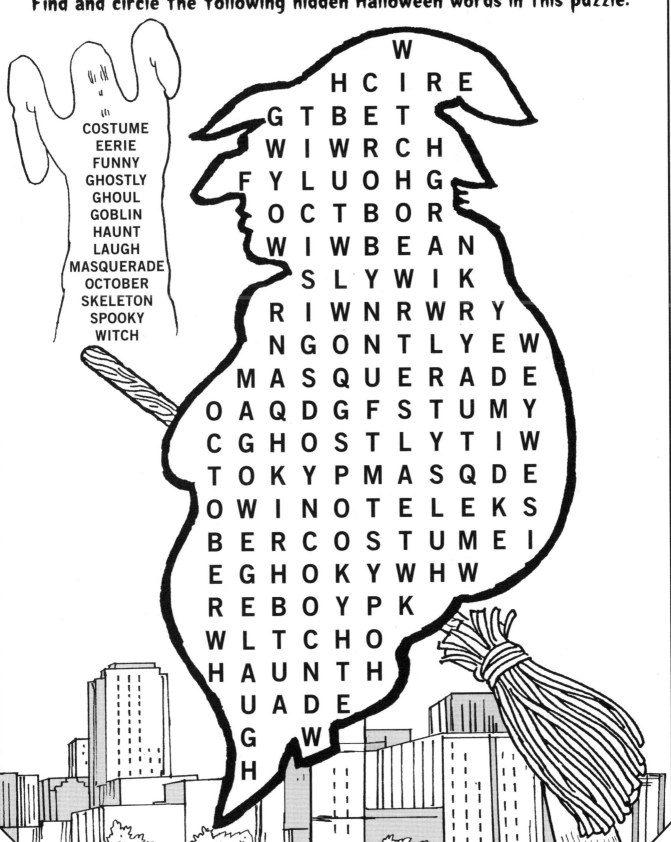

```
              W
        H C I R E
      G T B E T
    W I W R C H
  F Y L U O H G
  F O C T B O R
  W I W B E A N
    S L Y W I K
    R I W N R W R Y
    N G O N T L Y E W
  M A S Q U E R A D E
  O A Q D G F S T U M Y
  C G H O S T L Y T I W
  T O K Y P M A S Q D E
  O W I N O T E L E K S
  B E R C O S T U M E I
  E G H O K Y W H W
  R E B O Y P K
  W L T C H O
  H A U N T H
  U A D E
  G H   W
```

CREATING WORDS

Can you make at least 25 words using the letters from the word
HALLOWEEN ?

*Write
your
words
here:*

DOT-TO-DOT

Who is this mystery trick-or-treater?
Complete this dot-to-dot picture to find out!

START 1.
2
23
3
22
4
21
20
5
19 18 6 7
17 8 10
16 9
15 11
14 12
13

9

ESCAPE THE GHOUL

Can you pick the correct path in this maze and escape the clutches of this Halloween ghoul?

FIND AND COLOR

Can you find and color 13 witch hats hidden in this tree?

11

FOLLOW THE FOOTPRINTS

Can you follow the correct path of footprints to reach the trick-or-treat bag?

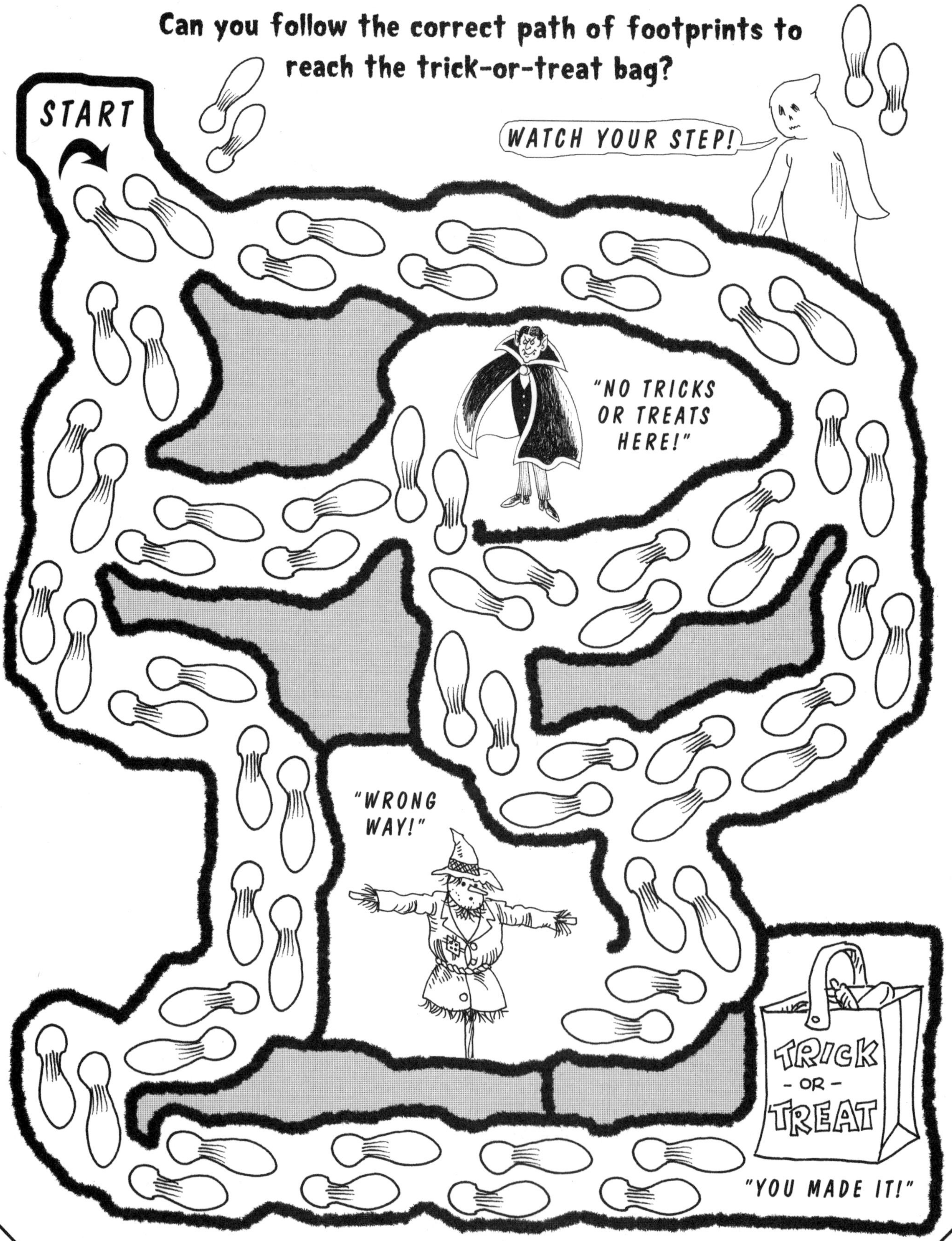

START

WATCH YOUR STEP!

"NO TRICKS OR TREATS HERE!"

"WRONG WAY!"

TRICK
- OR -
TREAT

"YOU MADE IT!"

GHOSTLY RIDDLES

Help "Wally the Werewolf" discover the answers to these ghost riddles. Write the letters of the alphabet that come BEFORE each of these letters.

What kind of music do ghosts like?

___ ___ ___ ___ ___ ___   ___ ___ ___   ___ ___ ___ ___ !
S   I   Z   U   I   N   B   O   E   C   P   P   T

How do ghosts turn on their computers?

"   "
___ ___ ___ ___   ___ ___ ___ ___
U   I   F   Z   C   P   P   U

___ ___ ___ ___   ___ ___ !
U   I   F   N   V   Q

What do little ghosts have in their rock collections?

___ ___ ___ ___ ___ ___ ___ ___ ___ ___ !
U   P   N   C   T   U   P   O   F   T

What do ghosts drink on Halloween?

___ ___ ___ ___ ___ - ___ ___ ___ !
H   I   P   V   M   B   J   E

HALLOWEEN CLASSIC

Name this famous 19th-century American author,
best known for his classic short story
"The Legend of Sleepy Hollow."

START

NATHANIEL HAWTHORNE

EDGAR ALLAN POE

WASHINGTON IRVING

HALLOWEEN FUN FACT

Use this code chart to fill in the blanks below.

A	B	C	D	E	F	H	I
7	11	4	15	5	16	3	12

L	N	O	R	S	T	W	Y
8	1	9	13	2	14	10	6

My favorite holiday falls in the tenth month of the year.

H A L L O W E E N   I S
3 7 8 8 9 10 5 5 1   12 2

C E L E B R A T E D   O N
4 5 8 5 11 13 7 14 5 15   9 1

O C T O B E R
9 4 14 9 11 5 13

T H I R T Y - F I R S T .
14 3 12 13 14 6   16 12 13 2 14

15

HALLOWEEN LINK-UP

Write the name of each picture in the correct spaces.

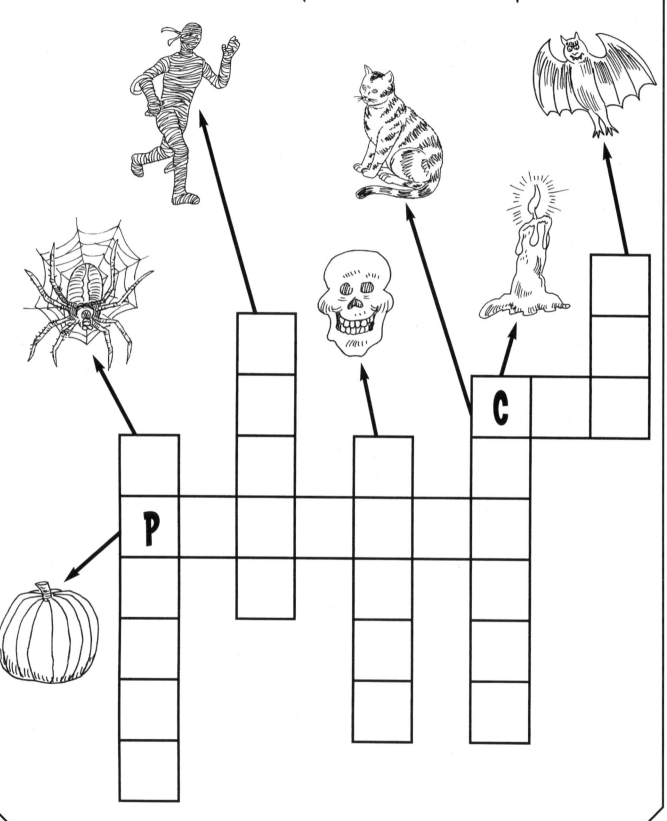

HALLOWEEN SPELL

Answer each clue correctly. Then write the numbered letters in their correct spaces at the bottom of the page to spell out a Halloween word.

PREHISTORIC CREATURE ___ ___ ___ ___ ___ ___ ___ ___
 5 $\quad$ 7 $\quad$ 11

___ ___ ___ ___ ___ OR TREAT
 3

SIXTH MONTH OF THE YEAR ___ ___ ___ ___
 1 $\quad$ 8 $\quad$ 10

A YOUNG CAT ___ ___ ___ ___ ___ ___
 4 $\quad$ 9 $\quad$ 12

A REACTION TO SOMETHING FUNNY ___ ___ ___ ___ ___
 6 $\quad$ 2

___ ___ ___ ___ $\quad$ ___ ___ $\quad$ ___ ___ ___ ___ ___ ___
1 $\quad$ 2 $\quad$ 3 $\quad$ 4 $\quad\quad$ 5 $\quad\quad$ 6 $\quad$ 7 $\quad$ 8 $\quad$ 9 $\quad$ 10 $\quad$ 11 $\quad$ 12

HALLOWEEN TRIVIA MAZE

Where did the first Halloween parade in America take place?
Correctly travel through this maze to reach the answer.

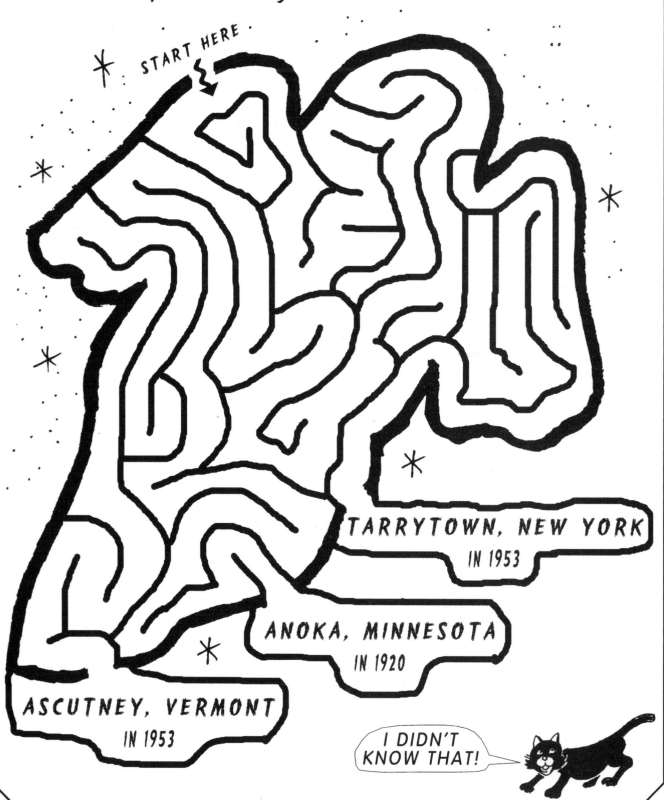

START HERE

TARRYTOWN, NEW YORK
IN 1953

ANOKA, MINNESOTA
IN 1920

ASCUTNEY, VERMONT
IN 1953

I DIDN'T KNOW THAT!

HAUNTED HOUSE MAZE

Choose the correct path to find your
way out of this eerie house.

HIDDEN ANSWER

Fill in the areas that contain a dot ● to reveal the answer to this riddle.
WHAT GAME DO GHOSTS LIKE TO PLAY?

HIDDEN MESSAGE

Write the name of each picture in every pumpkin in the correct spaces.
One letter from each will help spell out a hidden message.

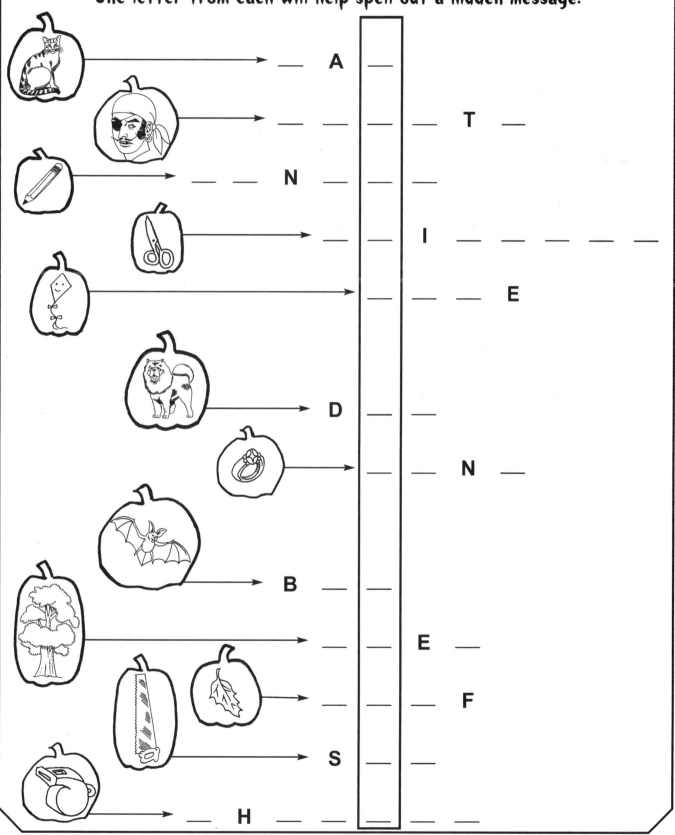

HILARIOUS HOUSE OF DR. FUNKANSTEEN

Can you find and circle the following hidden objects in this scene?

1 CARROT ☐ 1 DRUM ☐ 1 FISH ☐ 1 GHOST ☐
1 HAMMER ☐ 1 HOURGLASS ☐ 1 MOUSE ☐
2 PUMPKINS ☐☐ 1 ROLLING PIN ☐ 1 YO-YO ☐

JUST THE OPPOSITE

Write the opposite of each word. One letter from every word will help spell out a hidden Halloween phrase.

COLD ⟶ _ | _ O | _

EARLY ⟶ _ | _ | _ E

DOWN ⟶ _ | _ | _

BOTTOM ⟶ _ O | _ | _

NO ⟶ _ | _ | E _

SOFT ⟶ _ | _ R | _

SHORT ⟶ _ | _ L | _

FALSE ⟶ _ | _ E | _

START ⟶ _ | _ D |

SIT ⟶ _ | _ A | _

LEFT ⟶ _ | _ H _

OFF ⟶ _ | _

SMALL ⟶ _ I | _

23

LET'S COMPARE

Look closely at these two pictures. Find and circle 10 things that are different in the bottom picture.

LET'S DRAW

Draw exactly what you see in the numbered boxes at the top into the blank boxes of the same number below.

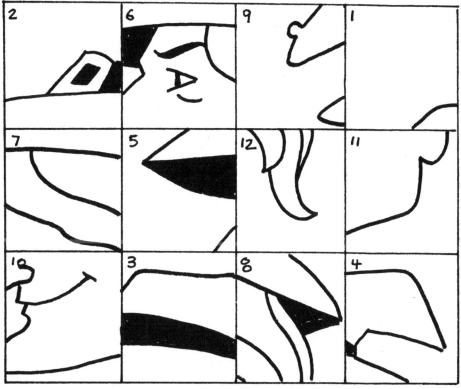

1	2	3	4
5	6	7	8
9	10	11	12

MYSTERY PATH MAZE

Enter the correct path with a dark pencil
to create a Halloween shape.

MYSTERY PICTURE

Draw exactly what you see in the numbered boxes at the top into the blank boxes of the same number below.

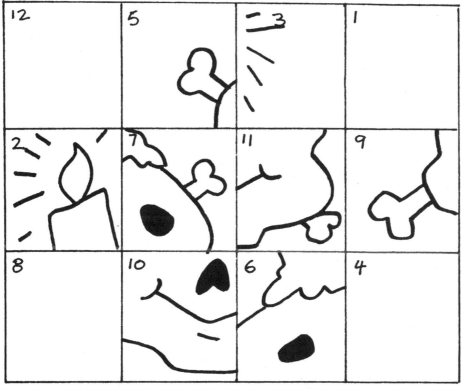

12	5	3	1
2	7	11	9
8	10	6	4

1	2	3	4
5	6	7	8
9	10	11	12

MYSTERY WORD LIST

Write the letters of the alphabet that come **BEFORE** each
of these letters to spell out the mystery Halloween word list.

1. ········ $\overline{T}$ $\overline{L}$ $\overline{V}$ $\overline{M}$ $\overline{M}$

2. ········ $\overline{U}$ $\overline{P}$ $\overline{N}$ $\overline{C}$ $\overline{T}$ $\overline{U}$ $\overline{P}$ $\overline{O}$ $\overline{F}$

3. ········ $\overline{N}$ $\overline{P}$ $\overline{O}$ $\overline{T}$ $\overline{U}$ $\overline{F}$ $\overline{S}$

4. ········ $\overline{H}$ $\overline{I}$ $\overline{P}$ $\overline{T}$ $\overline{U}$

5. ········ $\overline{Q}$ $\overline{J}$ $\overline{S}$ $\overline{B}$ $\overline{U}$ $\overline{F}$

ON THE LOOKOUT

Find and circle the following objects in this spooky scene.

4 BATS ☐☐☐☐   1 BOWLING PIN ☐   1 CANDLE ☐   1 FOOTBALL ☐
4 GHOSTS ☐☐☐☐   1 GUITAR ☐   1 MUSHROOM ☐   1 OWL ☐   1 SOCK ☐

PUMPKIN SEARCH

The word PUMPKIN appears 6 times in this
word puzzle. Find and circle each one.

I WAS
ONCE A
PUMPKIN!

```
P U M P N P
P U M P K I N
U M P N I K I
M P U M U P K
P K I N P M P
K I P K N U M
I N I K M P U
N I K P M U P
```

SCRAMBLED HALLOWEEN WORDS

Help "Frankie" unscramble these Halloween words.
The clues can help you.

E O T C U S M _ _ _ _ _ _ _

clue: *an outfit you wear to pretend you are someone else*

O N E E K S L T _ _ _ _ _ _ _ _

clue: *set of bones in a body*

U K I N P P M _ _ _ _ _ _ _

clue: *orange fruit that grows on a vine*

H O S T G S _ _ _ _ _ _

clue: *fictitious spirits who say "Boo!"*

F I C F N O _ _ _ _ _ _

clue: *wooden box a vampire might sleep in*

R S M N O T E _ _ _ _ _ _ _

clue: *make-believe creature like "Frankie"*

TWIN PIRATES

Every Halloween pirate on this page has an exact twin. Draw a line from each pirate on the left to her correct twin on the right.

UNLUCKY THIRTEEN?

The number 13 appears thirteen times in this haunted house scene. Can you find and circle each one?

WHAT'S DIFFERENT?

What is different about these two trick-or-treat scenes?
Find and circle 10 things that are different in the bottom picture.

WITCH TWO?

These six Halloween witches may appear the same ... but look closely as only 2 are identical. Find and circle the 2 witches that are the same.

1.

2.

3.

4.

5.

6.

A BATTY RIDDLE-MAZE

Travel through this bat maze to answer the following riddle.

"WHICH IS MY FAVORITE HOLIDAY?"

START

APRIL FOOL'S

HALLOWEEN

THANKSGIVING

page 1

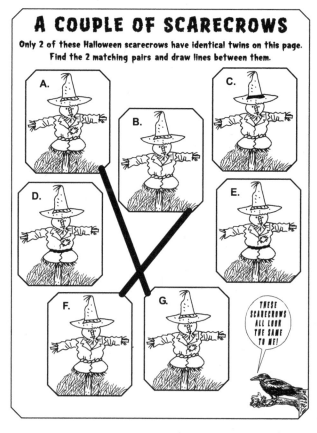

A COUPLE OF SCARECROWS

Only 2 of these Halloween scarecrows have identical twins on this page.
Find the 2 matching pairs and draw lines between them.

A.

B.

C.

D.

E.

F.

G.

THESE SCARECROWS ALL LOOK THE SAME TO ME!

page 2

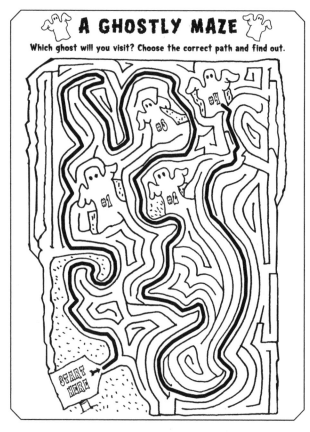

A GHOSTLY MAZE

Which ghost will you visit? Choose the correct path and find out.

START HERE

page 3

A PUMPKIN FACT

Use this special chart to decode the fact below.

A	B	D	E	F
H	I	K	L	M
N	O	P	R	S
T	U	V	Y	Z

PUMPKINS HAVE

INHABITED OUR

PLANET FOR

THOUSANDS OF

YEARS!

page 4

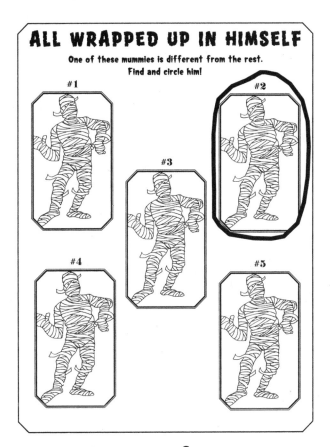

A TO Z DOT-TO-DOT

Complete this alphabet dot-to-dot picture.

A ——— Z

start

ALL WRAPPED UP IN HIMSELF

One of these mummies is different from the rest.
Find and circle him!

#1 #2 #3 #4 #5

page 5

page 6

CIRCLE-A-WORD

Find and circle the following hidden Halloween words in this puzzle.

COSTUME
EERIE
FUNNY
GHOSTLY
GHOUL
GOBLIN
HAUNT
LAUGH
MASQUERADE
OCTOBER
SKELETON
SPOOKY
WITCH

```
      W
  H C I T R E
G T B E T C H
W I I W R C H G
F Y L U O H G O
  O C T B O R E
W I W B E A N
  S L Y W I K R
R I W N R W R Y
N G O N T L Y E W
M A S Q U E R A D E
O A Q D G F S T U M Y
C G H O S T L Y T I W
T O K Y P M A S Q D E
O W I N O T E L E K S
B E R C O S T U M E I
E G H O K Y W H W
R E B O Y P K
W L T C H O
H A U N T H
  A U G H
  D E
  W
```

CREATING WORDS

Can you make at least 25 words using the letters from the word
HALLOWEEN ?

Here
are
just
a few:

ALL	LAWN
AWE	LEAN
AWL	LOAN
EEL	LONE
EON	LOW
HALL	NEW
HALO	NOEL
HEAL	NOW
HEEL	ONE
HELLO	OWE
HEN	OWL
HOLE	WALL
HONE	WELL
HOW	WHALE
HOWL	WHEEL
LANE	WHO
LAW	WON

page 7

page 8

DOT-TO-DOT

Who is this mystery trick-or-treater?
Complete this dot-to-dot picture to find out!

page 9

ESCAPE THE GHOUL

Can you pick the correct path in this maze and escape the clutches
of this Halloween ghoul?

page 10

FIND AND COLOR

Can you find and color 13 witch hats hidden in this tree?

page 11

FOLLOW THE FOOTPRINTS

Can you follow the correct path of footprints to
reach the trick-or-treat bag?

page 12

GHOSTLY RIDDLES

Help "Wally the Werewolf" discover the answers to these ghost riddles. Write the letters of the alphabet that come BEFORE each of these letters.

What kind of music do ghosts like?

R H Y T H M   A N D   B O O S !
S I Z U I N   B O E   C P P T

How do ghosts turn on their computers?

T H E Y   "B O O T"
U I F Z   C P P U

T H E M   U P !
U I F N   V Q

What do little ghosts have in their rock collections?

T O M B S T O N E S !
U P N C T U P O F T

What do ghosts drink on Halloween?

G H O U L · A I D !
H I P V M   B J E

page 13

HALLOWEEN CLASSIC

Name this famous 19th-century American author, best known for his classic short story "The Legend of Sleepy Hollow."

START

NATHANIEL HAWTHORNE

EDGAR ALLAN POE

WASHINGTON IRVING

page 14

HALLOWEEN FUN FACT

Use this code chart to fill in the blanks below.

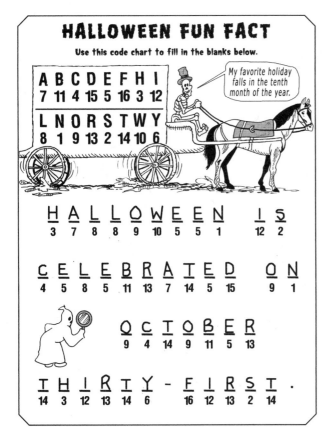

A	B	C	D	E	F	H	I
7	11	4	15	5	16	3	12

L	N	O	R	S	T	W	Y
8	1	9	13	2	14	10	6

My favorite holiday falls in the tenth month of the year.

H A L L O W E E N   I S
3 7 8 8 9 10 5 5 1   12 2

C E L E B R A T E D   O N
4 5 8 5 11 13 7 14 5 15   9 1

O C T O B E R
9 4 14 9 11 5 13

T H I R T Y - F I R S T .
14 3 12 13 14 6   16 12 13 2 14

page 15

HALLOWEEN LINK-UP ✏

Write the name of each picture in the correct spaces.

M U M M Y

S P I D E R

P U M P K I N

S K U L L

C A N D L E

B A T

C A T

page 16

39

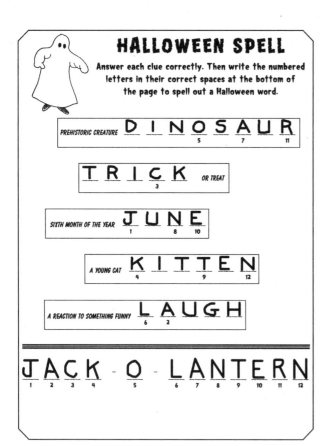

HALLOWEEN SPELL

Answer each clue correctly. Then write the numbered letters in their correct spaces at the bottom of the page to spell out a Halloween word.

PREHISTORIC CREATURE **D I N O S A U R**
5 7 11

T R I C K OR TREAT
3

SIXTH MONTH OF THE YEAR **J U N E**
1 8 10

A YOUNG CAT **K I T T E N**
4 9 12

A REACTION TO SOMETHING FUNNY **L A U G H**
6 2

J A C K - O - L A N T E R N
1 2 3 4   5   6 7 8 9 10 11 12

page 17

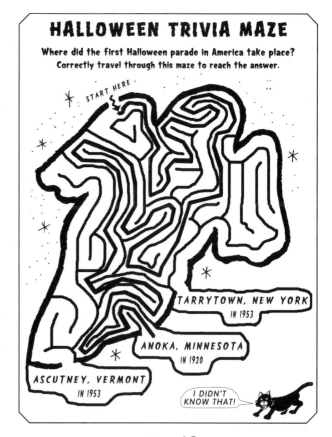

HALLOWEEN TRIVIA MAZE

Where did the first Halloween parade in America take place? Correctly travel through this maze to reach the answer.

START HERE

TARRYTOWN, NEW YORK
IN 1953

ANOKA, MINNESOTA
IN 1920

ASCUTNEY, VERMONT
IN 1953

I DIDN'T KNOW THAT!

page 18

HAUNTED HOUSE MAZE

Choose the correct path to find your way out of this eerie house.

GO BACK!!

YOU MADE IT!!

BOO! WRONG WAY!!

TRY AGAIN!!

TURN BACK!!

START HERE

WELCOME

page 19

HIDDEN ANSWER

Fill in the areas that contain a dot ● to reveal the answer to this riddle.
WHAT GAME DO GHOSTS LIKE TO PLAY?

HAUNT AND SEEK

page 20

HIDDEN MESSAGE

Write the name of each picture in every pumpkin - in their correct spaces. One letter from each will help spell out a hidden message.

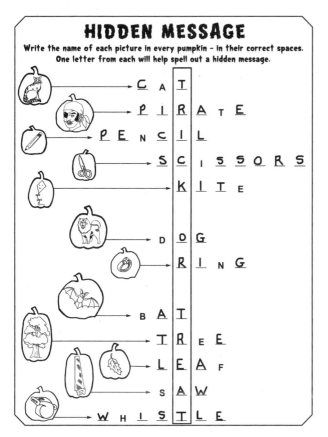

C A T
P I R A T E
P E N C I L
S C I S S O R S
K I T E
D O G
R I N G
B A T
T R E E
L E A F
S A W
W H I S T L E

page 21

HILARIOUS HOUSE OF DR. FUNKANSTEEN

Can you find and circle the following hidden objects in this scene?

1 CARROT ☐   1 DRUM ☐   1 FISH ☐   1 GHOST ☐
1 HAMMER ☐   1 HOURGLASS ☐   1 MOUSE ☐
2 PUMPKINS ☐☐   1 ROLLING PIN ☐   1 YO-YO ☐

page 22

JUST THE OPPOSITE

Write the opposite of each word. One letter from every word will help spell out a hidden Halloween phrase.

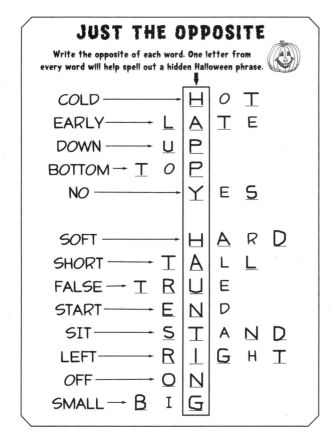

COLD — H O T
EARLY — L A T E
DOWN — U P
BOTTOM — T O P
NO — Y E S

SOFT — H A R D
SHORT — T A L L
FALSE — T R U E
START — E N D
SIT — S T A N D
LEFT — R I G H T
OFF — O N
SMALL — B I G

page 23

LET'S COMPARE

Look closely at these two pictures. Find and circle 10 things that are different in the bottom picture.

page 24

41

LET'S DRAW

Draw exactly what you see in the numbered boxes at the top into the blank boxes of the same number below.

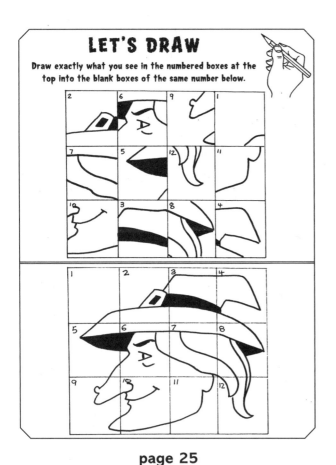

page 25

MYSTERY PATH MAZE

Enter the correct path with a dark pencil to create a Halloween shape.

What can it be?

BEGIN HERE

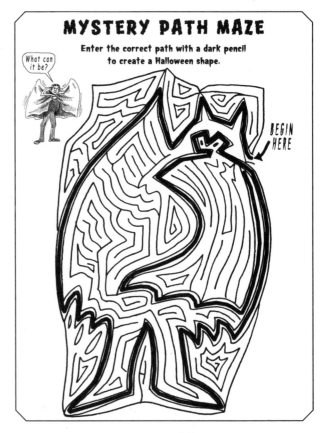

page 26

MYSTERY PICTURE

Draw exactly what you see in the numbered boxes at the top into the blank boxes of the same number below.

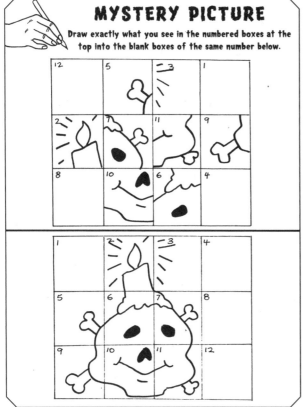

page 27

MYSTERY WORD LIST

Write the letters of the alphabet that come BEFORE each of these letters to spell out the mystery Halloween word list.

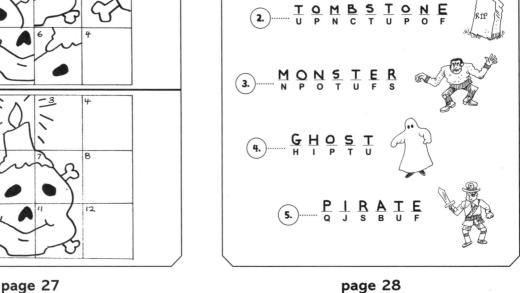

1. <u>S K U L L</u>
   T L V M M

2. <u>T O M B S T O N E</u>
   U P N C T U P O F

3. <u>M O N S T E R</u>
   N P O T U F S

4. <u>G H O S T</u>
   H I P T U

5. <u>P I R A T E</u>
   Q J S B U F

page 28

42

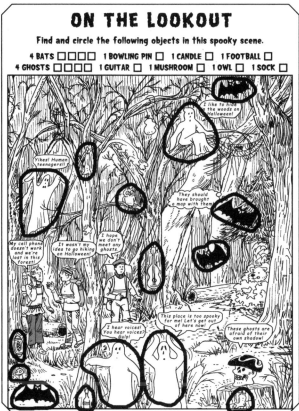

page 29

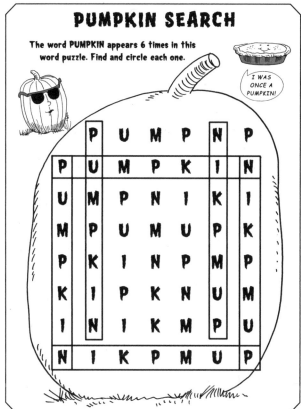

page 30

SCRAMBLED HALLOWEEN WORDS

Help "Frankie" unscramble these Halloween words. The clues can help you.

EOTCUSM <u>C O S T U M E</u>

clue: *an outfit you wear to pretend you are someone else*

ONEEKSLT <u>S K E L E T O N</u>

clue: *set of bones in a body*

UKINPPM <u>P U M P K I N</u>

clue: *orange fruit that grows on a vine*

HOSTGS <u>G H O S T S</u>

clue: *fictitious spirits who say "Boo!"*

FICFNO <u>C O F F I N</u>

clue: *wooden box a vampire might sleep in*

RSMNOTE <u>M O N S T E R</u>

clue: *make-believe creature like "Frankie"*

page 31

page 32

page 33

WHAT'S DIFFERENT?
What is different about these two trick-or-treat scenes?
Find and circle 10 things that are different in the bottom picture.

page 34

WITCH TWO?
These six Halloween witches may appear the same ... but look closely as
only 2 are identical. Find and circle the 2 witches that are the same.

page 35

44